Let's Get Along

Resolving Conflict

BY ALYSSA KREKELBERG

ABOUT THE AUTHOR

Alyssa Krekelberg is a children's book editor and author. She lives in Minnesota with her hyper husky.

The Child's World®
childsworld.com

Published by The Child's World®
1980 Lookout Drive • Mankato, MN 56003-1705
800-599-READ • www.childsworld.com

Photographs ©: Air Images/Shutterstock Images, cover, 1, 10, 13, 14; Jacob Lund/iStockphoto, 5, 6, 9; Shutterstock Images, 17, 18, 21

ISBN 9781503844582 (Reinforced Library Binding)
ISBN 9781503846784 (Portable Document Format)
ISBN 9781503847972 (Online Multi-user eBook)
LCCN 2019956592

Printed in the United States of America

Contents

CHAPTER ONE

Learning to Share

Ally and Jackson are baking a pie with their mom. Jackson grabs the rolling pin, but Ally takes it away. He has never used the rolling pin before.

"Do not touch the rolling pin," Ally says.

"You cannot do this part."

Jackson starts to cry. He looks away from Ally.

People should think about how their actions and words affect others.

5

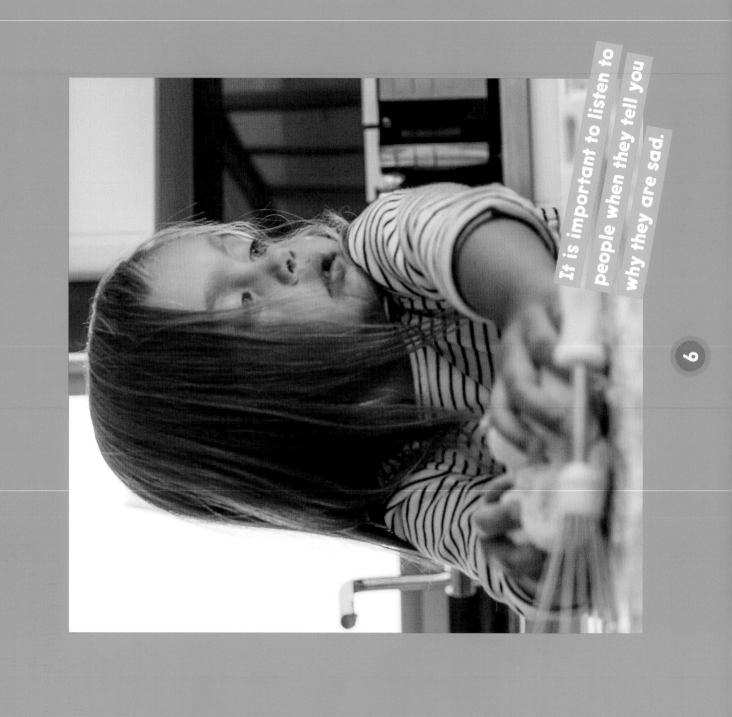

It is important to listen to people when they tell you why they are sad.

6

Ally is **surprised** by her brother's reaction. "What is wrong?" she asks.

Jackson says, "I am sad because you will not let me help."

Ally did not mean to make Jackson sad. She remembers a time when her mom did not let her help.

"I am sorry," Ally says. "Let me teach you how to roll the dough, too."

Ally and Jackson work together to make the pie. Jackson rolls dough. Ally mixes fruit and sugar. Their mom helps them with the oven. Ally and Jackson are glad they talked through their **conflict**.

8

Friends and family can work through conflicts to have fun together again.

Getting mad at people usually will not help you feel better.

10

CHAPTER TWO

Thinking about Others

Max does not play well during baseball games. He misses the ball when he tries to hit it. Some teammates yell at Max. They call him names.

During their next game, Max does not take his turn at bat. James wonders why his friend Max is not playing.

James smiles and asks if Max is OK.

Max says that he gets **nervous** and upset when he does not play well.

James thinks about how he would feel if he were Max. He would not want to play baseball if it made him upset.

If your friend seems sad or upset, you should ask how they are feeling.

13

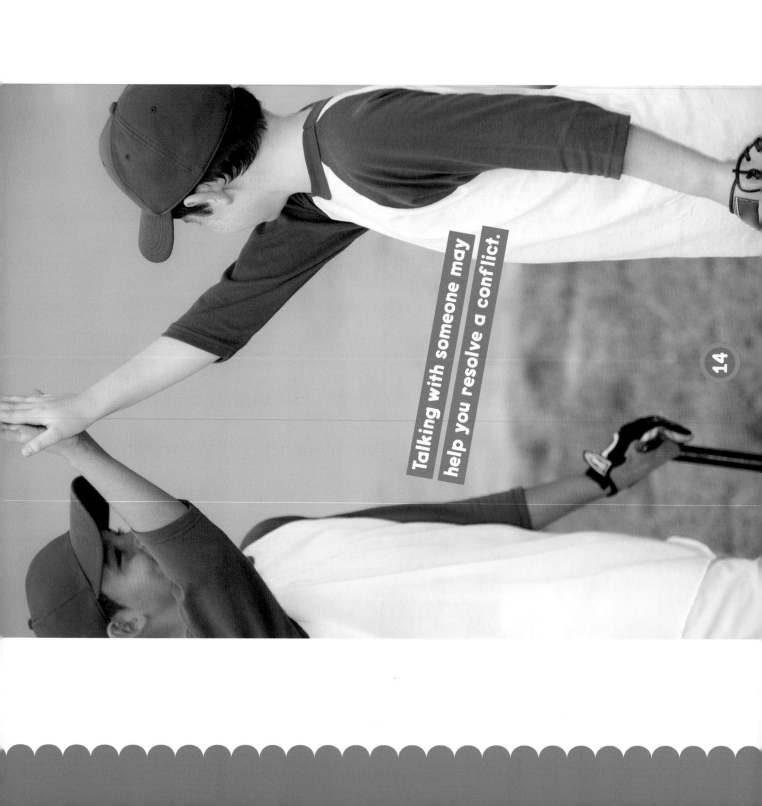

Talking with someone may help you resolve a conflict.

14

"Let's practice together," James says.
"That way we can both get better. We should also talk to the team about hurting your feelings."

Max smiles and gives James a high five. He is glad that James is such a good friend.

CHAPTER THREE

Conflict with Friends

Molly and Sasha are playing in the snow.

Then Sasha walks away.

Molly is **annoyed** that Sasha left. She wants to yell and stomp her feet. Instead Molly takes a deep breath. Molly thinks about how she would feel if Sasha yelled at her. She would feel sad.

Sometimes friends do not agree on everything.

17

If you are upset with your friend, try talking to him or her about your feelings.

18

Molly wants to understand why Sasha left. She walks over to Sasha on the playground. "It hurt my feelings that you left me alone," Molly says.

"I am sorry. I did not think about how it would make you feel," Sasha says. "I wanted to play on the playground."

The friends make a **compromise**.

They play in the snow for ten minutes.

Then they play on the playground. Molly

smiles. She is glad that she and Sasha

resolved their conflict.

When is a time you did not agree with a friend?
What did you do to avoid a fight?

How would you compromise with a friend?
Explain your answer.

A compromise is a great way
to make people happy.

21

GLOSSARY

annoyed (uh-NOYD) To be annoyed is to feel angry or to have lost patience. The team was annoyed with Max.

compromise (KOM-pruh-mize) Compromise means to agree on something that is not exactly what you wanted, but meets some of the wants of others. Molly and Sasha reached a compromise.

conflict (KON-flikt) A conflict is a serious disagreement between people. Molly and Sasha resolved a conflict.

nervous (NER-vuss) If someone is nervous, that means he or she is worried about something. Max gets nervous when he does not play well during baseball.

surprised (sur-PRIZD) To be surprised is to not expect something is going to happen. Ally was surprised that she hurt her brother's feelings.

TO LEARN MORE

Books

Haley, Charly. *Worried*. Mankato, MN: The Child's World, 2019.

Riley, Elliot. *LaLa Does (Not) Like to Share*. Vero Beach, FL: Rourke Educational Media, 2019.

Smith, Bryan. *What Were You Thinking? A Story about Learning to Control Your Impulses*. Boys Town, NE: Boys Town Press, 2016.

Websites

Visit our website for links about resolving conflicts:
childsworld.com/links

23

INDEX